YOUR KNOWLEDGE HAS VALUE

- We will publish your bachelor's and master's thesis, essays and papers

- Your own eBook and book - sold worldwide in all relevant shops

- Earn money with each sale

Upload your text at www.GRIN.com and publish for free

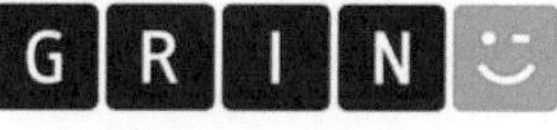

Sandra Kuberski

Gandy, Canaletto & Hogarth in the "Picture Room" of the Sir John Soane's Museum in London

GRIN Publishing

Bibliographic information published by the German National Library:

The German National Library lists this publication in the National Bibliography;
detailed bibliographic data are available on the Internet at http://dnb.dnb.de .

Imprint:

Copyright © 2012 GRIN Verlag GmbH
Print and binding: Books on Demand GmbH, Norderstedt Germany
ISBN: 978-3-656-85992-5

University of Essex,
Academic Year: 2011/12, Autumn Term,
Module: AR111 (Art, Sex and Death in the Eighteenth Century)

Presentation by Sandra Kuberski

The "Picture Room" in Sir John Soane's Museum in London

INTRODUCTION

Today I'm talking about a selection of paintings in the picture room of Sir John Soane's Museum in London. In the previous presentation we have already heard that the specialty of the picture room is its exceptional hanging with the openable panels.

In this way the room that actually measures about 13 to 12 feet can grasp over a hundred paintings. Another advantage of the panels is that like this it is possible to see the paintings in different angles.

Most of the paintings were bought by Soane on auctions, some are also commissions by himself.

GANDY

In fact, the first paintings that entered the collection of Soane were collected and commissioned as adjuncts to his collection of architectural pieces.

From 1798, Joseph Michael Gandy worked nearly 30 years as draughtsman for Soane. Like Soane, he had been to Rome and as Gandys own career as architect was rather unsuccessful, he merged his talents with those of Soane. To present his ideas and drafts to those people responsible for the construction of a building, Soane commissioned exceptional paintings in settings like a jungle or other fantasy landscapes which of course was a clever way to advertise his work. The drawings combine correctness of detail with lots of theatrical effect.

An example is the painting which shows a "Selection of public and private buildings" and is located on the south side of the picture room. The painting was exhibited at the Royal Academy in 1818 and shows over 100 of Soane's buildings, either as models or paintings. In the center we see a model of the Bank of England, which is illuminated by a lamp.

On the left side in the shadow we see the façade of the Soane museum. Next to it is the tomb that Soane designed for his wife who died in 1815, it's veiled by a black blanket.

In the right foreground, Soane is sitting at a desk, depicted in his role as architect, nearly buried by his work, but as he is surrounded by piles of items and objects, also in his role as collector. The room symbolizes the home of Soane which was turned into a museum, where hardly any space was left without a collected piece.

The passion of collecting paintings increased over the years, especially around the turn of the century, when he bought his house Pitzhanger Manor in Ealing. This gave him more space for his collection, and from now on (as we have already heard) he was a keen visitor of auctions.

CANALETTO

In 1796 Soane made his first important purchases, two **Canaletto** paintings, in 1807 he bought a third Canaletto.

The paintings show different perspectives of Venice, like the canal or the famous bridge. But the paintings are not mere landscape paintings, they also show the hustle and bustle of everyday life.

The most striking thing about those paintings is their clarity, the bright blue sky that is very dominant. The public buildings that are shown, are depicted in a very detailed and accurate way. As viewer one is really drawn into the scene and can imagine how it is to be there.

HOGARTH

The last decade of his life, Soane's collecting interest focused on works by his contemporaries at the Royal Academy. Many paintings in his collection where commissioned by himself.

It was his aim to encourage an independent British School of painting, which could free itself from outside influences, for example French and Italian history painting.

The most known components of Soane's collection are the two series by William Hogarth, "A Rake's Progress" and "An Election", which he did not commission but bought them on auctions.

William Hogarth was a one of Britain's most prominent artists in the 18th century. His works are satires of contemporary England, always a harsh criticism of society. Hogarth was a keen observer of his cultural, political, and social surrounding and translated those observations into caricature-like artworks.

In Soane's days the paintings were still considered to be very racy. After a sensitive lady visitor complained about scenes with drunken men and revealing prostitutes, which apparently made her feel faint, Soane came up with the idea of the panels and in future the works were only shown to male visitors on demand. [1]

Short Introduction to the *Rake's Progress*:

The series deals with a young man called Tom Rakewell, who after the death of his father inherits his fortune. But unfortunately Tom Rakewell lives a very extravagant life and soon he loses all of his money. In this scene we see him drunk at the Rose Tavern, a brothel in Covent Garden, surrounded by prostitutes.

Even after he is arrested for debt he does not change his life and gets married to an old rich lady.

In the gaming house, the Rake loses this second fortune as well.

Again, the Rake ends up in prison, now becoming insane. And so, in the final scene he is just about to die in the madhouse, surrounded by other victims of insanity.

AN ELECTION

Hogarth loves it to integrate playful details or allusions in his paintings. It takes awhile to look at the paintings, and to discover every detail. It seems that Soane really enjoyed those works. This shows his sense of humour and political opinion.

An even better example is the second series called **"An Election"**, which hangs in pairs on the outer planes of the north and south cabinets.

The series alludes to the Oxfordshire election in 1754 and was painted in the same year. But it can be seen as depiction of a typical election in the 18th century. The series does not serve to show a specific historic event, but rather to unveil political and aristocratic wrongs.

---

[1] http://www.timetravel-britain.com/articles/london/soane.shtml

Hogarth wanted to startle the viewers and the paintings are easy to understand for everybody, not only an elitist audience.

On the one hand they are amusing for the eye, but on the other they also engage with the mind of the spectator, want him to think about the topics, society, his own life.

First Painting: **An Election Entertainment**

The opening scene of the series is set in an inn, we see a political banquet by the Whigs in anticipation of the election. Bricks are thrown in by members of the opposing Tory party and the people inside try to beat back.

Second Painting: **Canvassing for votes**, shows political corruption.

The headquarters of each party are located in taverns. The Tory headquarter, called the "Royal Oak" is located on the left. The headquarter of the Whigs in the background can be recognized by the large crown sign in front of the tavern.

In the middle we see a farmer who is being bribed by the host to dine there by representatives of both camps. Ridiculously, he accepts bribes from both men at the same time.

At the inn in the background a fight has broken out, and two men are dragging down the inn sign with a rope. A third man knees on the beam over the sign and is sawing through it. The funny thing is that he doesn't seem to realize that when the sign (the crown) falls, he will fall as well.

Third Painting: **The Polling**

In the third painting we see a polling booth and in front of it a crowd of people.

In front of the booth we see a mentally disabled man in a chair, behind there's man wrapped in a white blanket, obviously dying or already dead. There was the anecdote of a corpse who actually cast a vote, so this can be seen as allusion to it. All the voters are somehow disabled. On the left side we see a coach, which is said to be an allegory. On the coach door we see the Union Jack, which reveals it as "coach of Britannia", the personification of whom is looking out of the window, alarmed by the happenings. The coach has broken down, but the two coachmen are busy gambling, but in fact are cheating mutually.

Fourth Painting: **Chairing the Member**

On the last painting we see the victorious party, the Torys, on their triumphal march through the town. The first candidate is carried on a chair, but the carriers come into conflict with some protesting people and the candidate is on the brink of falling down. In the left foreground we see the Whig party members, viewing the spectacle of the disruption of the triumph of their opponents with delight.

This painting is particularly chaotic, still really interconnected.
In the middle we see a sow and pigs, they have run over a woman and perhaps the carrier as well, who is moreover struck by the weapon of the man in the white shirt. The stroke was actually meant for the man in the front with the wooden leg, who is the owner of the bear that steals from the panniers of the man on the donkey. On the back of the bear sits a dressed monkey with a gun, two kids on the wall splash it with water.

Rehanging

As mentioned before although Soane wished his collection to stay as he "left" it, some changes were made to the original arrangement.
For example, in 1890 the Canalettos were moved to a so-called New Picture Room in order to provide better access for artists who wished to copy it. In 2011, they were returned to the original position, above the fireplace.

Bibliography

A New Description of Sir John Soane's Museum, 11th Revised Edition (Marlborough: Libanus Press, 2007).

Darley, Gillian, *John Soane: An Accidental Romantic* (New Haven: Yale University Press, 2000).

Britton, John, *The union of architecture, sculpture, and painting: exemplified by a series of illustrations, with descriptive accounts of the house and galleries of John Soane* (London: Oxford University, 1827).

http://www.soane.org

Dubrulle, Hugh, Food for Thought: The Humours of an Election (http://www.anselm.edu/academic/history/hdubrulle/ModernBritain/text/gradingandassignments/food/fdwk01b.htm, 30/04/12).

Sir John Soane: The Art and Mind of an Art Collector, interview with Will Palin, Assistant Curator of Sir John Soane's Museum from 2009 (http://robefish.wordpress.com/2009/05/09/sir-john-soane-the-art-and-mind-of-an-art-collector, 30/04/12).

Pearman, Hugh, *John Soane's magician: the tragic genius of Joseph Gandy* (http://www.hughpearman.com/2006/09.html, 30/04/12).